Personal Revival

Living the Christian Life
in the Light of the Cross

Stanley Voke

Publishing

P.O. Box 1047
Waynesboro, GA 30830 USA
Tel: (706) 554-1594
Fax: (706) 554-7444
gabriel@omlit.om.org

This edition, Gabriel Publishing 2002.

ISBN: 1-8845-4305-7

Cover design: Paul Lewis
Cover photo: Stephen Punton
Impreso en Colombia
Printed in Colombia

Contents

Foreword

*T*his is a very readable little book. Quite clearly the author has a real gift of being able to express that which is profound in simple, practical, every-day language. The reader will find it instructive and helpful.

At the same time in every page of it there is a personal challenge to personal revival. In clear and forthright language the way into the fulness of blessing is revealed to be by the path of confession and cleansing. How much we all need to put the label 'sin' where God puts it, for only then can there be victory.

I pray that this book will receive a wide circulation and that it's message, which is so urgently needed in these days, will bring immeasurable blessing to countless people.

Alan Redpath

Preface

*A*s I traveled by train through Central Wales I noticed through the carriage window many thousands of tiny streams flowing down the slopes and hills on every side fed from heavy rains that fell day after day in the region around. As they linked with one another, they grew in size and strength until on reaching lower areas they flooded a large town.

The streams of God are flowing today! In many places there is a spiritual movement in the hearts of Christians who pray that God will revive His work in the midst of the years, and long in the words of an old hymn -

Oh, for the floods on the thirsty land,
Oh, for a mighty revival.

My idea of revival had always been of some spiritual flood that would somehow, some day, come from God. I had no thought of the streams that might cause it until one day I met a man from Africa who had been in a revival. He came at a time when, barren in my ministry and defeated in my life, I longed for God to revive the Church, yet laid the blame for lack of blessing on everyone except myself.

It was his simple testimony that impressed me. He claimed only to be a needy sinner, yet his face shone with peace and joy as he spoke of the

Lord Jesus and the power of His precious blood to cleanse day by day. Soon God began to convict me, causing me to repent of one thing after another until my wife and I together with others in the church found ourselves walking a new path of penitence and fellowship, hesitatingly at first, sometimes even unwillingly. But God faithfully showed us where and how we needed to come back again and again to the cross. The streams of grace had begun to flow and one result is this book.

For twelve years now we have been learning to know our need and prove the wonder of the grace of God, so that the sinner's place has become familiar ground, though alas we have often sought to avoid it. But it has become the ground of grace where heaven is opened and the light of God shines on us. As we have come there with others, Jesus Himself has drawn near and gone with us so that we have discovered a new sweetness in fellowship and a new simplicity in revival.

God's streams are flowing everywhere today amongst Christians who long for reality, who hunger for God and cry out for the Holy Spirit to move among men that the spiritual need of the hour may be met. We find groups for prayer, fellowship and Bible Study forming in many places. There is a new sense of need and repentance and a willingness for fellowship on a level that underflows all denominational barriers. This may well be the most significant spiritual event of our time. The streams of life are flowing! Will they lead to God's floodtide?

There are many who believe we shall experience a great spiritual revival before Christ returns. We can only say that it is always the will of God to bless His church if she is willing to repent and seek His face. If we are ready in the day of His power, He will be gracious in the day of our need. Of this we can be sure that as in those hills of Wales, however small the streams, if there are enough and they flow together, the flood will come.

The danger is, they may not flow together. In fact they will flow apart if we emphasize things that confuse because they contradict. Frustration in the church always produces those who cry 'Lo, there', leading us to streams that are not safe because they are not centered in Christ. That is why the Gospel is such a sure way, for it is the way of grace for sinners, including saved sinners, who repent. It is Jesus Himself we need — Jesus the Fountain of Life springing up in our souls to flow out in rivers of living water. This is the secret of the fulness of the Holy Spirit, for He seeks only to glorify Christ. What is given in this book is the experience of personal revival, found at the cross of Christ as we have come, bringing our continual need to be met by the One who is Himself Revival. As we have come to the fountain of cleansing we have found the Fountain of Life.

Stanley Voke

Like water, God's love flows down to the lowest place.

1

The way up is
the way down

*"Never further than Thy cross,
Never higher than Thy feet."*

*T*his book is about the greatest thing in the
world — the grace of God for sinners who repent,
which is the love and power of God in action on
behalf of needy people. It must therefore of ne-
cessity be a book about human need because
grace is not grace unless it is related to need.
Like water, God's love flows down to the lowest
place.

The little parable in Luke 14 about the man
who sat in the wrong seat has always interested
me. I imagine him arriving at the great wedding
reception before most other guests and looking
round hopefully for a seat. Presently seeing a
comfortable one near the head of the table he
decides on it. The other guests arrive until all
seats are filled except one — the lowest of all,
which after a while is quietly taken by a man
nobody appears to notice.

Finally the host arrives and looking round the
company calls for a distinguished person whose
name everyone knows. To the surprise of all he
is found sitting in the lowest seat, whilst our
friend who first arrived is discovered sitting in
the very seat reserved for this important man.
Imagine his confusion as he is told to give place

9

to this man and finds to his shame that he must go down to the lowest seat of all.

It may surprise us to know that we are all like this man because we all like to go up. In some cases this appears in positive ways. We push for the best seats, we like to be given honor, to be treated with respect, to rise in the estimation of others. It is only natural!

For most of us, however, it may be shown in negative ways in that we do not like to be passed over. Indeed, we may be resentful for years because we were not elected to some position or treated as we thought fit by someone else. In no matter is this so evident as in our dislike of criticism. We do not mind suffering want, pain or persecution, but we do not like criticism from others, whether just or unjust. The fact is we want to live above criticism — in the highest place.

Many of us want to be successful Christians. As we read our Bible or look at others we long to live on a higher plane of life. It may be that like the man in the parable we think we have arrived there, so we sit contentedly in our chair of spiritual achievement. Or quite understandably we aim at a higher place, like the lady who came to me saying, "Well, I have become a Christian, I have been baptized, I have been made a church member, and now I am a Sunday School teacher. What is the next thing?" Her idea of the Christian life was a kind of ladder of achievements and appointments to be slowly ascended. It is natural to think that the way up is up.

How different was the Lord Jesus! Like the important man in the story He came into the world taking the lowest place. At birth, in baptism, in all His ministry He took this place, even kneeling on one occasion with a towel and a bowl at His disciples' feet, placing Himself on a lower level than they that He might wash their feet. Nowhere was He lower than at Calvary, for there He was numbered among the transgressors, and accepted both the criticisms of men and judgments of God for sins that were not His own. He truly sat at the lowest place, nor did He seek a higher, and when we try to be above criticism, we try to be above Christ.

He humbled Himself to the manger
And even to Calvary's tree,
But I am so proud and unwilling
His humble disciple to be.

The Bible is full of the records of those who in their pride have tried to climb to the highest place. We read of Lucifer who sought to reach to the mount of God only to be cast down to hell. Pharaoh, Nebuchadnezzar, Simon Magus and the Pharisee in the temple tell the same story. Paul tried to climb a ladder of merit and good works only to be brought down to the cross. All who seek to exalt themselves through pride will be abased by God because there is only One who is worthy of the highest place and that is Jesus.

We are all like this man.

Kneeling with a towel and
a bowl at His disciples'
feet

All that exalts itself above Him will be brought
down. That is what happened to the man in the
parable, as he was made to give place to another.

THE WAY UP IS THE WAY DOWN

There was only one way for this man — the
way down to the lowest place of all. Yet did he
but know, this was the very place where grace
could reach him. In fact the story suggests another occasion when he would be found taking
this place only to hear the host say to him,
"Friend, come up higher. The way up was the
way down, which is always God's way of blessing.

Joseph reached the place of glory by going not
up but down. As he walked the way of rejection
and humiliation without even a word of com-
plaint he little realized how every step brought
him nearer the fulfillment of his glorious
dreams. We read too of Mephibosheth finding
grace and wealth at the hand of David not by
trying to be anything in himself but by coming

down and staying there. He claimed to be no more than a dead dog and a servant, yet he was numbered among the king's sons and ate continually at the royal table.

Zacchaeus had to come down from his tree to find salvation. Peter came down from his boat to walk on the water to Jesus. Lepers and blind men came down to the Lord's feet to find healing. Prophets and apostles found the fulness of the Holy Spirit as they lay prostrate before God. The last church in Revelation was promised righteousness and riches when she took the place of poverty, blindness, nakedness and need. In each case, the way up was the way down.

This is why we emphasize penitence and brokenness. We cannot give place to the Lord without ourselves taking the lowest place. "Thou begin with shame to take the lowest place," says the Lord in the parable. We must *begin* somewhere. Many have been so busy seeking the higher place we have never even *begu*n to take the lower that we might receive grace. This lowest place is the sinner's place, where we see every other man as better than ourselves, because we are down in the dust before God. This is where we must come if grace is ever to reach us.

THE FOCAL POINT OF GRACE

There came a time when the same man who had put himself in the highest place was found sitting willingly in the lowest only to find to his surprise that grace reached him there in a wonderful way. It was as though the very One whose place he once usurped rose from His high seat to come beside him and say, "Friend, I once sat here instead of you. I was once scorned by all and

made lowest of the low. Now you have come here
of your own accord. Come and sit with Me. My
Father, the Host, is calling you to come higher."
The man whose sin once put him in the lowest
place now finds that grace brings him to the
highest.

In experience we have continually to take this
lowest place. Having once taken it we are willing
to take it again and again, yet paradoxically as
we sit there it is to find that Jesus meets us, and
we are in fellowship with Him even in heavenly
places.

The Christian life is one of victory and com-
pleteness in Christ, but the trouble is we forget
it is in CHRIST. We want to be strong in ourselves,
popular and powerful like Absalom, rather than
poor and crippled like Mephibosheth, who was
obliged to live by the grace of King David. We
think Christian success means a dynamic exu-
berance that is never in any kind of need.

For a Christian to be found in the lowest
place, repenting and confessing his need, seems
to us to be wrong. We think it is a negative

*"To this man will I look,
even to him that is poor and
of a contrite spirit, and
trembleth at My word!"*

attitude of introspection and defeat. We want to live in a higher place — higher than the feet of Christ. Many years ago we came there but we are there no longer. We have gone up on our own accord and are not now poor in spirit or found mourning for sin. We have forgotten that God says, "To this man will I look, even to him that is poor and of a contrite spirit, and trembleth at My word."[1] Perhaps this explains why we are cold and hard of spirit, when others who come to the cross are found free and full of joy.

In a certain place where God gave a remarkable revival there remained one church wholly unaffected. It seemed hard to believe it was so, until one day a visitor asked an old Christian why. She looked up at the building, then shook her head sadly and said four words — "Too high! Too high!" Is this our trouble, that we are too high for the Lord? We have climbed to the highest place when we ought to come down to the lowest. We have built up ground within ourselves until we are standing far above the sinner's place. We need the Holy Spirit to show us the Lord Jesus taking the lowest place for us, so

Too high! Too high!

that we with shame may begin to take it too.
Then we shall come in our hearts to the place
where grace can reach us and every possible
blessing of God becomes ours. The way down will
become the way up — into fellowship with our
exalted Lord, and the fulness of His Holy Spirit.

Reference:
Isaiah 66:2.

2

The sinner's place

"Nothing in my hand I bring,
Simply to Thy cross I cling."

*T*he hardest thing for anyone is to take the sinner's place. So hard in fact that many never take it at all, while others, having once been brought there, do not care to come there again. for none are by nature fond of the sinner's place.

Yet if we do not come there we cannot really know Christ or taste the sweetness of God's forgiving grace. If we avoid it we are as good as saying we have no sin and so deceive ourselves.

TAKING THE SINNER'S PLACE

The sinner's place is where we accept without excuse that we are sinners. We may admit only one sin such as jealousy or pride, we may be convicted of something that seems small but in so doing we have come again to the sinner's place, though we may have been Christians for many years. Behind that one sin God may show us things more serious until not one but many things are admitted and we are brought to admit the whole radical evil of our nature. A man once confessed he had stolen a rope. He brought it back, but the next day he came again, this time bringing a cow he had been unwilling to admit was on the end of the rope! When we take the sinner's place we admit the truth about

17

A man once confessed he had stolen a rope ...

ourselves — the whole truth.

The sinner's place is where we take blame. We stop excusing ourselves and saying: "I was not really myself when I did that." Instead we bow our head saying: "Yes, Lord, that was me, that is what I am really like." We no longer blame our nerves, our circumstances, or other people.

... there was a cow on the end of the rope!

Should someone point out some fault or criticize us, even unkindly, we do not argue and justify ourselves or try to explain things away. We even admit to the critic that if he knew us as we really are he would find much else to criticize. We save endless time and breath when we come quickly to the sinner's place. Indeed things would be different in many a church if the members met regularly there.

This is the place David took as, when Nathan challenged him, he bowed his head saying: "I have sinned." Here Job stood and cried, "Behold, I am vile," and Isaiah said, "Woe is me! for I am undone." Here the publican prayed, "God be merciful to me a sinner," here Peter fell at the feet of Jesus saying, "Depart from me, for I am a sinful man." In this place the prodigal son confessed: "Father, I have sinned and am no more worthy." Paul often knelt in the sinner's place and many a saint has watered it with his tears. If we have not come here we have not yet begun with God.[1]

We do not like the sinner's place for it is most humbling to our pride. I once had a strange dream. My pride had been hurt over some petty issue at home and I went to bed with a hard heart. In the dream I was on a great height, far below my family stood calling on me to come down. I did not know how to do this until I saw a great tree stretching its branches up as though inviting me to step on them and thus be lowered to the ground. But I was afraid of being hurt so I stayed on my lofty height, lonely and proud and cold. When I awoke I realized the tree was the cross of Jesus, and as I came to it in repentance I found peace and fellowship once more. I was afraid of being hurt! That is why we do not like the sinner's place. We are afraid of hurting our pride, so we fight, argue, put others in the wrong, excuse ourselves, in fact do anything rather than take the sinner's place where God awaits to forgive and set us free.

So I stayed on my lofty height, lonely and proud and cold.

AVOIDING THE SINNER'S PLACE

Often we avoid this place because we will not call sin, sin. We talk of shortcomings, failures, weaknesses, frailties, faults, disabilities, propensities; anything but sin. A rose by any other name is just as sweet, and sin by any other name is just as evil — to God. The trouble is we make our own definitions instead of accepting God's. In the Scripture sin is anything short of the glory of God, anything that misses the mark of moral perfection or crosses the line of God's will, anything that is twisted from the plumbline of divine righteousness whether it be in motive, desire, intention, instinct, thought, habit, look, word, deed, reaction or relationship. If done heedlessly or in ignorance it is still sin and to call it something else needing neither repentance nor forgiveness is to avoid the sinner's place.

We can refuse to see sin as sin. Maybe we are active people who have no time to bother with such trivialities. We have our positions and programs to maintain. Like Naaman we are busy winning our laurels while we cover our leprosy. We address meetings, chair committees, take on jobs, give money to this and that, in fact, do anything except confess ourselves spiritual lepers who need, as others, to wash and be clean. We are as those in Jeremiah's day who rushed like horses into battle but never stopped to repent or say, "What have I done?" We are so very busy — too busy ever to stand in the sinner's place.[2]

We may avoid this place by assuming the role of correctors. With our doctrines neatly tied up we are evangelical experts with a keen sense of theological smell. We love to correct but not to be corrected. Like the Pharisees of old we keep ourselves out of the sinner's place by putting others in. We are so full of knowledge that we have no room for a broken and contrite heart. Yet even Henry Martyn, great saint as he was, recorded in his diary, "I have resolved never to reprove another except I experience at the same time a peculiar contrition of heart!" He found he needed to live in the sinner's place. We may avoid this place by making our security in Christ a pretext for non-repentance. We are assured of our salvation, yet somehow we are no longer convicted of sin. We are like the small boy who when sent from the table to wash his hands returned with a big smile and the astonishing remark, "Well, they've had such a wash this time they'll never need to be washed again."

Eternal security in Christ is a great and grand truth. We are by faith the sons of God, and the citizens of heaven. But we are still sinners and always shall be. We still need to wash at 'The fountain opened for sin and for uncleanness'.[3] Grace will never lead us into sin, but it will ever convict us of it, and sin thus revealed will always lead us back to grace.

It is possible to avoid the sinner's place by misapplying the blood of Christ, speaking of it as 'covering' or 'protecting' as did the blood of the Passover lamb. The sacrifice of Christ on Calvary, however, was for sin. It is an atoning, not simply a protecting agent. If therefore we need it, we do so as sinners coming for cleansing, not as sinless ones needing only to be secured from evil outside ourselves. When we speak only of the blood protecting us we are avoiding the sinner's place.

One of Spurgeon's students once preached before him on the 'The Whole Armor of God'. A conceited young man, he dramatized his message, putting on the armor piece by piece, until having fortified the whole, he waved the sword of the Spirit and cried triumphantly, "And where is the devil now?" at which Spurgeon leaned forward and said, "Young man, he's inside that armor!" We must watch we do not let Satan in by forsaking the sinner's place. Our hearts are deceitful above all things and like the mythological Proteus will adopt any guise to hide their true nature. Beneath our spiritual phraseology and church reputation we are but poor sinners, who need to be cleansed every day in the blood of Jesus.

FINDING GRACE IN THE SINNER'S PLACE

Is it not strange that the place we sinners avoid is the very one the sinless Savior took? Surely if He were the Son of God He would have come down from the cross! Miracles, mighty sermons,

He who insists he is right will be pronounced wrong.

even resurrection itself we could expect of such a
One, but not a baptism in Jordan with publicans
and harlots, or a criminal execution with murderers and thieves! Yet this is where He came, for His
face was set towards this place from all eternity.

There on the same level a sinner met Him
that day. Unlike his comrade who died blaming
others and cursing God, this dying thief admitted guilt and found forgiveness. Peace and paradise came to him as he took the sinner's place
and found Jesus there. This is the paradox of
grace. He who insists he is right will be pronounced wrong, while he who admits he is wrong
will be declared right. The righteousness of God
is only given to those who stand in the sinner's
place.

Here and here alone is the place of true peace,
for here we cease our strivings and find our God.
Here is rest of heart and heaven's door. Here we
cast away our pretense, and admit what we
really are. Here we come to Jesus to be cleansed
by His precious blood. Here the Holy Spirit fills
and holiness is found. Here are the springs of
revival. This is where the whole church needs to
come again and again. It is the place of truth and
grace and freedom — the sinner's place. When
were you last there? In fact, are you there now?

References:
1 - 2 Samuel 12:13; Psalm 51:4; Job 40:4; Isaiah 6:5;
    Luke 18:13; Luke 5:8; Luke 15:18.
2 - Jeremiah 8:6.
3 - Zechariah 13:1.

3

The plumbline of God

"Just as it is in Thy pure eyes
Would I behold my heart."

We all agree that the church needs to be revived. But how does revival begin? Must we wait for another Wesley or Finney or look to this or that new movement? Shall we pray on and on for a revival which may never come? Or can the church be quickened today as Lazarus was raised because Jesus was and is now the Resurrection and the Life?

As the line hung straight it showed up every crooked place in the wall.

Revival begins with God when God begins with His people. Any study of revivals will show that spiritual awakening has begun when Christians under the conviction of the Holy Spirit have come to the sinner's place and begun to repent. But the question is, how are we brought to this place of repentance? It would seem John Wesley had the answer when he said to his preachers, "Preach first the holiness of God." It is this we need today — a new vision of the holiness of God.

THE PLUMBLINE

Amos was a prophet who had some extraordinary visions. In one he saw God standing like a man on the top of a wall holding a line at one end of which was a weight. As the line hung straight it showed up every crooked place in the wall and the message came, "Behold, I will set a plumbline in the midst of My people."[1] Let us see this picture of God standing over our lives with His plumbline, because this shows us how and where revival begins. It is by God's plumbline we are put in the sinner's place.

What is the plumbline, you ask? Isaiah tells us it is the righteousness of God. "I will make judgment the line, and righteousness the plummet."[2] Now righteousness simply means 'that which is straight', and we cannot possibly know whether a thing is straight unless we have a perfect standard by which to judge. Every builder uses a level and a rule. Every clock is checked by Big Ben. Life would be chaotic if we had no standards. It is like this in the spiritual and moral order. God has His standard or plumbline by which He measures all things. One writer calls it "that norm to which men and things should conform and by which they are measured. What this is depends on the nature of God."[3]

This nature of God is clearly shown in the Bible. We do not altogether find it in the natural world, nor do the religions of men help us very much. But the law and commandments of the Old and New Testaments show the true moral nature of God; for instance, in the Ten Commandments or the Sermon on the Mount. More and more clearly this nature of God is seen until it is fully shown in Christ who is the Image of God. His perfect life of love and truth, meekness and majesty, service to man and devotion to God is like a plumbline set beside the crooked wall of our sinful lives. In the words of Whittier:

We own Thy sway, we hear Thy call,
We test our lives by Thine.
Thou judgest us, Thy purity
Doth all our lusts condemn.

THE TEST OF THE PLUMBLINE

We see God standing on the wall of our life looking upon every part of it. As He holds the plumbline against us, it becomes obvious where things are not quite straight. We look at Him, but He is not hard or unkind. His eyes are full of love as gently He shows us where we are crooked and need to be made straight. He must do so for He is holy and righteous, and cannot do otherwise.

Thy kind but searching glance can scan
The very wounds that shame would hide.

Every part of life is touched — for instance our *thought life*. The Psalmist knew this when he said, "Thou understandest my thought afar off ... and art acquainted with all my ways."[4] As we think in our hearts so are we; therefore this is a most important realm. God knows all about it and has His standard for us. He tells us to think things that are honest and true and just and pure and gracious, to have the mind that was in Christ Jesus, lowly and loving and self-emptying. We are to think on His law day and night, to have a mind that is spiritual and to bring every thought into captivity to Christ.

Then the plumbline goes deeper — into our *motives*. It tests whether we have a single eye to the glory of God, whether we do everything for the glory of the Lord or to please men. It searches out if our ruling passion be the love of God — for God and for others — whether all we do is in faith and sincerity, whether our motives are mixed so that pride rules our will and selfishness governs all we do.

Then it touches our *speech*. How much the Bible says about this! How searching it is! Our speech is always to be with grace, seasoned with salt. We are to be kind yet wise. No corrupt talk, whether idle, evil, malicious or impure, is to come out of our lips. We are to bridle our tongues so that we speak what edifies others and ministers grace to our hearers.

Have you ever listened back on a tape recorder to a conversation, say at a meal table, which you did not know was being recorded? It can be an experience to shame you! Yet Christ is the silent Listener to every conversation and the Day of Judgment can record back every word we have said.

What does God say of our *bodies* as He holds His plumbline to us? He says we are not our own, but our bodies are members of Christ, temples of the Holy Spirit. They are no longer instruments of sin but vehicles of righteousness, every member of which is to be yielded to Him.

In our *homes* too the plumbline hangs as it sets the standard of Christ for our domestic life. Husbands are to love their wives as Christ loved the Church; wives are to be as the church is to Christ — adorned with a meek and lowly spirit. What a standard is this! As for children, they are to obey as in the Lord — even as Jesus Himself at Nazareth. Parents are to be to their children as God is to us. Indeed there is no loftier pattern than is set for our home life, for it is based on the very relation of the Persons of the Trinity one to another.

As we come to the *church* we find God measuring things there. Our love for each other is to be like that of Christ for us; we are to consider others better than ourselves, to be of one heart and mind, and to lay down our lives for the brethren. We are not to deceive or judge or malign or defraud but in all things to be pure-minded, tender-hearted and open-handed with one another.

In *business* we are to be honest, diligent and considerate to all. In *the world in general* we are to be blameless and harmless, shining as lights, acting like salt to purify and preserve good, while at the same time keeping ourselves unspotted from every evil.

Having held the line against each part of the wall it is as though God then measures our own relation to Him by showing that we are to love Him with all our heart and soul and strength and mind. We are to seek Him always, honor Him in all things and find in Him our chief delight.

WHAT THE PLUMBLINE DOES

In the light of these things how crooked we are! I have heard of primitive people who think in curves so that all they build is round and even their seeds are planted in a curve. We have our own ideas of what is right; that is why we need the plumbline to show us where we are twisted. Often we make ourselves into plumblines and become so good at measuring everyone else's wall that God cannot show us ours. When He does, we may refuse to admit we are crooked or cover up our irregularities with plaster of our own.

God goes on quietly holding the plumbline against the wall showing us that we are full of iniquity. This word means 'that which is crooked', which 'deviates from the plumb'. It means we are all unequal to God's standard and however much we may criticize others or excuse ourselves, yet in His sight our walls are as crooked as one another's. So the plumbline humbles us and brings us in repentance to the sinner's place.

If this were all it did, we should be condemned. But God points us away from our crookedness to One who was altogether straight and we hear the prophet Isaiah saying, "All we like sheep have gone astray... and the Lord hath laid on Him the crookedness of us all."[5] The One who was utterly straight because He was the Holy One of God took all our twistedness to His cross, so that repenting and believing we might be made straight. Just there where we are shown to be out of plumb, even to a small degree, we may repent and be covered and made straight again.

A little girl once took a liking to some of her father's new books. When he was out she would creep into his study, take them from the shelves and strew them over the floor. She was told to leave them alone but it made no difference. Finally there came a warning of punishment. The next day she came in again and was busy taking the first book when she heard a sound, and turning round saw her father watching her from his desk. She looked wildly, took the book, dropped it, then rushed across the room to bury her head, sobbing, in her father's arms. Gathering her up he kissed her tears away and gave her a hug. She never touched those books again.

So God searches us with His plumbline not to drive us into judgment or despair, but to draw us sweetly to repentance that in His arms we might find forgiveness and the fulness of His love. He wants us not to hide from Him but in Him, and it is this we learn to do when we come to the sinner's place. Then it is that revival begins in our hearts. Have we learned this yet?

References:
1 - Amos 7:8.
2 - Isaiah 28:17 (R.V.).
3 - *Snaith* - Distinctive Ideas of the Old Testament.
4 - Psalm 139:2.
5 - Isaiah 53:6.

4

The broken and
the contrite heart

"Blest are the men of broken heart
Who mourn for sin with inward smart.

We were saying farewell at the station to a
servant of God who had been used in many parts
of the world. "Good-bye, brother," we said. "We
shall pray that you may be used and blessed
wherever you go." He looked at us and said,
"Pray only one thing for me — that I may always
be broken." He knew only too well that this was
his greatest need. It is ours as well. That I may
always be broken!

OUR NEED FOR THE BROKEN SPIRIT

By nature we are all unbroken. We are part
of a world where men push each other around,
because what matters is the big and the important, a world where pride and power and person-
ality count for everything. In the mildest of us
there is pride and the love to be king in our own
right. On the level of the world this is thought
right and proper. But we who are Christians
belong to One who was meek and lowly of heart,
who gave Himself to be broken on the cross. He
was not concerned about important positions.
But we are, so that when God has to deal with
us, His greatest problem is not our sin (for He

32

dealt with that on the cross) but the hardness
and unbrokenness of our hearts. Here is the root
of our trouble.

Unbrokenness is a fearful thing. It is the very
spirit of the devil whose nature is so full of
incurable pride that he can only resist God forever. He is the exact opposite of the Lord Jesus
who always does the Father's will.

The Scriptures are full of stories of unbroken
people, men like Pharoah and Nebuchadnezzar
and King Saul whom God had to break in judgment. It tells us of men like Jacob and Moses and
David, whom God had to break before He could
bless them. It shows too how David sinned with
a high hand when he once took another man's
wife, then resorted to deceit and finally murder,
to cover his sin.[1] How for a long time he was hard
and unrepentant until God in mercy broke him
and brought him to the sinner's place.

WE MUST BE BROKEN BEFORE GOD

God knows how much we need to be broken,
so He uses people or situations to humble us that
we might be brought wounded and helpless to
the foot of the cross. We learn to praise Him for
it when afterwards we see it was the best and
kindest thing He could do, for it was the only
thing we needed. Some people are broken in a
wrong way; they are broken on the wheel of life
only to become bitter and resentful until in their
hardness they curse the God of heaven.

We need to understand the difference between the sorrow of the world which produces
death and godly sorrow which produces repentance.[2] There is a false brokenness in which we
are sorry for ourselves because the world has

been hard on us. There is a true brokenness when God has so dealt with us that we are truly sorry for our sin. This kind of sorrow produces repentance and brings no regret. As the Psalmist puts it, "The bones which Thou hast broken rejoice."

It was like this with David. While his heart was hard he became increasingly miserable, for God's hand, he said, was heavy upon him and his moisture was turned into the drought of summer. Then came the prophet Nathan to challenge him about his sin and warn of its consequences. Finally, his little child died and David was completely broken, yet behind it all was the Lord dealing lovingly with him, making him truly contrite so that with Job he could say, "God maketh my heart soft."[4] It is a wonderful thing when God does this.

WE MUST BE BROKEN ABOUT SIN

For some time it seems David went on trying to worship God but the joy of his salvation had gone. God had become so unreal that his soul was dried up like a piece of parched ground. While he was in this state Nathan came with his story about the rich man who had stolen the poor man's lamb. David flared up in anger and ordered that this rich man should die. This is always our reaction when we are hard and impenitent. We see and judge in others the very sin we are refusing to acknowledge in ourselves.

At that point God began to break David. He showed him how this other man's sin was really his own; how while he had wronged others — Bathsheba, Uriah, his own family and people and even himself — it was really God he had

wounded, the God who had given him everything
and whom he professed so much to love. He
showed him too how another had to die because
of his sin, even the innocent child who had been
born because of it. I think it was this that
brought David at last to a broken spirit. Beyond
the murdered soldier and the stricken mother,
beyond the sick child and the stern prophet, he
saw God, sad and displeased, so that in anguish
he cried out, "Have mercy upon me, O God. My
sin is ever before me. Against Thee, Thee only
have I sinned."[5]

True brokenness means we are brought to the
end of ourselves before God. We see our sin in the
light of God, see what it has done to Him and how
another Child was born to suffer and die because
of it. We see how the spear of our pride and the
nails of our lusts have pierced Him, the Son of
God, and yet how that very piercing on the cross
only brought forth the precious blood to cleanse
us, His very murderers. It is seeing Calvary that
breaks our hard hearts. It is here our stubborn-
ness is melted, our rights are renounced, and we
stand stripped of our glory and foolish pride.
Here we can claim nothing but sinnership and
ask nothing but mercy. Wesley says:

"Neither passion nor pride
   Thy Cross can abide,
But melt in the fountain
   that streams from Thy side:
Come then from above,
   its hardness remove,
And vanquish my heart
   with the sense of Thy love.

GOD'S SACRIFICE AND HOME

On the cross Jesus was completely broken.
Some of His last words to His disciples about
Himself were, "This is My body which is broken
for you." One of the final things about His death
was that 'He bowed His head'. It was the sign of
what He had done to an infinite degree. Indeed
the most precious thing to God about His beloved
Son was His brokenness. Have you ever noticed
that each time God openly declared His approval
of His Son by speaking from heaven it was when
Jesus was committing Himself to the cross? The
first time was when He stood meekly in Jordan
to be baptized with sinners as the Lamb of God.
Then came the Voice and the Dove as God saw
mirrored in the heart of His Son that cross on
which He was to be broken for us.

When God looks into our hearts He often finds
hardness and unbrokenness which is not the
spirit of Jesus, but of Satan. He sees pride and
self-esteem with which He can have nothing
whatsoever to do. So He has to break us. Then
when our hearts are contrite He sees something
like Christ, something corresponding to His own
nature, which is the result of His work of grace
in us. We are in the sinner's place, offering the
sacrifice of a broken and contrite heart, and
whatever others may do, God does not despise it.
It is in fact the only ground on which He can meet
us. He calls it His sacrifice and His dwelling
place. "I dwell with him that is of a contrite and
humble spirit, to revive the heart of the contrite
ones."[6]

In a family where God had taught much of
this, a little girl of five was naughty one day.
When reprimanded she grew hard and finally in

Waiting until my heart gets soft again.

a temper rushed from the house and disappeared down the garden. Some while later a search was made and she was found sitting in a lonely place on a wall gazing across a field. "What are you doing up there?" she was asked. Tears came into her eyes as she said, "Waiting until my heart gets soft again that I may go and tell Mummy I am sorry." So it is with us, when we see the Lord Jesus so that our hearts are melted at Calvary, we find it easy to get right with others.

GOD'S BASIS OF BLESSING

How God blessed David! Out of his brokenness

came repentance and forgiveness and restoration. Solomon was born and two great penitential psalms written for all the world to read. The broken bones rejoiced as the joy of salvation was restored and David sang once more. It is always the same. Jacob, broken at Jabbok, was found limping, but he limped into the sunrising — a man with a new name and a new nature who lived in the blessing of God. Broken by God, he did not mind bowing to his brother even seven times, coming nearer each time. What a wonderful picture is this of the fellowship of those who are broken. We do not find it hard to break to one another when we have broken to God.

Often we are afraid of being broken. We think we are going to lose something, to be unmanned and unmade, as though God would rob us of the best. It is not like this at all; in fact, precisely the opposite. God blesses all He breaks. Victory came to Gideon's army when the pitchers were broken to release the light within them. Fulness came to the five thousand when Jesus broke the loaves that seemed so few. Fragrance poured through all the house when a box of ointment was broken over the Savior's feet. It all happened in the breaking. But when the Son of God was broken in the darkness and disintegration of the cross, Satan was overthrown, sin was dealt with, the Gospel set free and eternal life released for all the world. Calvary proves the principle that God always blesses brokenness, for He brings life out of death.

One day, standing in a potter's house, I looked at a large box full of soft pieces of broken clay, mere scraps from the potter's wheel. I asked what he did with them and whether he threw them away. "Indeed I do not," he replied, "they

I looked at a large box full of soft pieces of broken clay.

are too valuable. As long as they can be softened no broken pieces are ever thown away." Then we watched him take them to mould and soften them in his moist and powerful hands until like a miracle we saw the formless clay rise within those faultless fingers into a perfect shape — the vessel that was to be! It was broken clay but precious! Full of possibility while it was broken! "To this man will I look," says the Lord, "even to

We watched him take them to mould and soften.

him that is of a contrite spirit."[7] What a wonderful God He is!

References:
1 - 2 Samuel 11.
2 - 2 Corintians 7:10.
3 - Psalm 51:8

4 - Job 23:16.
5 - Psalm 51. (R.S.V.)
6 - Isaiah 57:15. (R.V.)
7 - Isaiah 66:2.

We saw the formless clay rise

... into a perfect shape

5

The end of the struggle

"Jesus, Thy blood and righteousness
My beauty are, my glorious dress."

A small boy came home one day from Sunday
School and said, "Mom, we had a new hymn
today. It said that Jesus knows all about our
struggles." Then pensively he added, "You know,
that isn't right. We don't struggle. Only snails
struggle."

This reminds me of a caption I once saw in a
missionary magazine. It showed a snail crawling
and a bird flying, under which were the words,
"What are you — snail or bird?" Some African
Christians, blessed at a convention, were seen
going home singing, their faces shining with joy.
Others said, "Look at those Christians — they
are like birds flying." But they themselves knew
how different it could be when their hearts were
not right with Jesus. Then they could be like
snails, earthbound, selfbound, struggling instead of soaring.

If we see only the plumbline putting us in the
sinner's place so that we remain in the state of
feeling sinful, we shall be like snails — struggling. Seeing sin does not set us free — we need
to see Jesus. For every one look at sin, said
Murray McCheyne, take ten looks at Christ.[1]
Then indeed we are like birds that fly.

THE STRUGGLE FOR RIGHTEOUSNESS

J.B. Phillips translates the fourth verse of Romans 10 by saying, "Christ means the end of the struggle for righteousness," thus throwing light on the Authorized Version: "Christ is the end of the law for righteousness." There is in all of us a struggle to get and keep our own righteousness, which is why it is so hard to come to the sinner's place.

This struggle is as old as Adam and Eve who, when charged with sin in Eden, at once put the blame on one another and finally on the serpent, while at the same time they made garments of fig leaves to give themselves some sort of covering from the holy eyes of God. By the time of the New Testament, the struggle was well under way, for the whole Jewish religion was a developed attempt to achieve righteousness by works. Of the Jews of his day, Paul said, they were ever "going about to establish their own righteousness,"[2] rather than submit themselves to the righteousness of God.

We are all the same. Have you ever watched children build a sand castle on the beach before an incoming tide? Frantically they heap up their walls, patting the soft sand into solidity and reinforcing it with sticks and stones only to see it washed away at the last. So we go round and round to establish our defenses against the waves of other people's criticisms. For some of us life becomes one long struggle to be what we know all too well we are not.

THE STRUGGLE FOR ATTAINMENT

One phase of this battle for our own righteousness is the struggle to reach a standard of perfection. We have seen how the plumbline of God holds us to a perfect standard and the danger is that life may become a prolonged attempt to reach it. We become Christians under law instead of grace, so that instead of living in peace, we are torn with tension. Sometimes we set the standard ourselves by picturing the kind of Christian we ought to be. We follow an ideal image in our minds. It is as though we see the man we ought to be standing on some lofty height calling us on as we struggle vainly up the slopes, yet he never lends us a helping hand.

Of course other people set the standard for us too. Everyone can tell us what we *ought* to be. We hear sermons and read books showing us the kind of Christians we should be, which only makes us feel guilty if we are sensitive, and self-satisfied if we are not. People put us on pedestals expecting this and that of us until life becomes one long struggle to be what others demand. So we live on under law trying to keep up to standards, while behind us is God's relentless law never letting us off; never lifting us up.

Are you a Christian living under law? Living under continual condemnation because you feel all the time you ought to be a better Christian, who prays more, does more, gives more? You are chained to a moral yardstick. You live under a yoke and a burden when all the while Jesus wants to give you rest.

THE STRUGGLE TO KEEP OUR REPUTATION

Another aspect of this struggle for righteousness is the fight for reputation. We are all reputation-conscious. Some of us have a reputation — it may be for piety, efficiency, leadership,

What are you — snail ...
or bird?

preaching, housekeeping, anything! Others of us
wish we had a reputation. Once acquired, or
assumed, it can haunt us, dog us, browbeat us,
wear us to shreds. Bondage to reputation can be
sheer slavery, and yet did we but know, it is only
a form of struggle for our own righteousness. We
are unwilling to be known as failures along any
line.

THE STRUGGLE FOR APPEARANCE

The struggle for righteousness consequently
becomes the struggle for appearance which simply means that somewhere we end up with being
dishonest about ourselves. Y once heard a man
speak to children about eggs. He had three of

them with labels attached. One egg was stale and it told us it was not what it used to be. The second was half-hatched and it announced it was not what it hoped to be. But the third was rotten and although it looked good, was honest enough to tell us it was not what it *seemed* to be.

Is it not true that we seem to be what we are not, like the Jews whose struggle for righteousness led them inevitably into hypocrisy? The trouble with success is that we dare not be failures for if we are to keep our reputation we cannot admit ignorance or sin. That would be to collapse the sand castle before the tide had even come in. It is better to struggle on even to breaking point than admit some need that would mean others knowing us as we really are.

The tragedy of all this is the idea that we find favor with God by reaching standards. This is precisely where we are wrong. Again Phillips' translation helps us in Romans 10, verse 5: "The man who perfectly obeys the law shall find life in it" — which is theoretically right but impossible in practice. If we could attain God's standard we should be blessed. But we cannot, so we end by being cursed. The very law that was designed to give us life has become the means of death, not because there is anything wrong with the standard itself, but because we sinners are unable to reach it.

CHRIST — THE END OF THE STRUGGLE

What a relief it is when we see Christ as the end of all this. He is the end of the struggle for righteousness since He not only fulfilled the law for us, but was cursed for us as well. He has not only attained our perfection but atoned for our imperfection. There is nothing more to struggle about, for He has done all for us and God asks nothing now but our repentance and faith.

All the fitness He requireth
Is to feel your need of Him

How beautifully Joy Davidman puts it: "the only way to get rid of a sin is to admit it. Without honesty, repentance and forgiveness and grace are not possible. ...the Christian is the only man who does not go around all the time feeling guilty. For him, sin is a burden he can lay down; he can admit, repent, and be forgiven. It is the unfortunate creature who denies the existence of sin in general, or his own in particular, who must go on carrying it forever. ...The way to freedom, however, was shown us long ago; it consists in the honest confession and repentance that alone can open our hearts to the Comforter"[3] To open our souls to God's grace means He not only saves us from being the people we are, but changes us into those we ought to be.

How easy it is! The only way to get rid of sin is to *admit* it! Why is this so hard? Surely because it means letting go of our own righteousness which is the very thing we do not like doing. Yet how can we have Christ's perfect robe of righteousness if we insist on keeping our own? It is impossible.

Jesus is our perfect righteousness. When we come to Him we need no other. The struggle for righteousness is over and He becomes our reputation and glory. We need not fear to come to the sinner's place, for when we do, it is to cease from our own works, to stop trying to be what we are not and admit instead what we are. At that point we accept Christ's own righteousness, we are justified before God and enter into peace. This is God's basic blessing for us, and the only true way of peace and joy.

> *Cast your deadly doing down,*
> *Down at Jesus' feet.*
> *Stand in Him, in Him alone,*
> *Gloriously complete.*

References:
1 - Memoir and Remains, p.252.
2 - Romans 10:3
3 - Smoke on the Mountain - Joy Davidman.

6

Finding grace in
the sinner's place

*"Plenteous grace with Thee is found,
Grace to cover all my sin."*

I remember standing once on the seashore looking at a desolate scene. The tide was out and as far as one could see there was nothing but ugly black rock and seaweed. A few hours later all was changed, for everywhere was glistening blue and white, while the rocks and weeds were gone. The tide had come in and covered them from view.

It may be that we have seen something of the ugliness of sin as we have been brought to the sinner's place. It is like that black seaweed in contrast with the beauty of the ocean. We feel so condemned and unfit for God, yet try as we may, we do not seem able to alter ourselves any more than we could move those massive rocks. Thank God, we do not have to. He is able to cover our sins by His grace as the waters cover the sea.

Grace is God's attitude to sinners by which He does for them what they do not deserve and in them what they cannot achieve. It is God Himself working in love and power both *for* us, *in* us and *through* us. It is God planning, providing, revealing. It is God active in history and experience on behalf of needy people. Grace was seen in Jesus Christ as He came into the world humbling Himself to the manger and the cross. It is

48

seen in the Holy Spirit as He comes to sinful people to cleanse and change them. Grace is God doing for us what we cannot do for ourselves and charging us nothing for it. It is God taking sides with us when He ought to be against us; God paying our debts and making us rich beyond compare; God making us what we could never be of our own accord. Grace is the most wonderful thing there is about God.

GOD MEETS OUR SIN WITH HIS GRACE

We do not know how great is evil until we see it in the light of God's holy law, for the law, we

Our sin is like that black seaweed in contrast with the beauty of the ocean.

are told, came into the world that "the offense might abound".[1] This does not mean that the Ten Commandments were given to make people sin, but that when the law of God is applied to us its effect is to show up sin. It stirs our conscience. It may even bring to activity the evil within us as the warmth of the sun rouses a dormant snake. That is why the law can never save, for it can only make sin apparent while it does nothing to help the sinner. A policeman, however kind, cannot help you if you commit an offense. He can only charge or arrest you as the case may be. The law exists to bring sin to light and the more we know of God the more we will be made aware of sin.

A young convert once came to me very puzzled because before his conversion he had thought himself very good but since conversion felt himself to be very bad. He thought he should have felt better not worse. The fact was the light of God shining in his soul was showing him what he was really like. It is perfectly true that

They who fain would serve There best
Are conscious most of wrong within.

God knows all about this and since we can only be doomed by His law He deals with us on a different basis altogether by meeting us with His grace, for that is our only hope. This is where the Lord Jesus comes in.

Jesus was grace incarnate! Think how He received and forgave a poor defiled Magdalene, or set free a devil-possessed man with whom no one could live. Look how He called to the hated little tax-gatherer up in his tree to come down that he might find salvation in his own house. All the dealings of Jesus with sinners were in grace. It streamed through His words, shone in His actions, even streamed through His clothes.

With what grace He bore with the disciples, forgave Peter in the very moment of his denial, prayed forgiveness on His murderers, called

Judas His friend and promised Paradise to a dying thief. Yet this was only the beginning, for when the Holy Spirit came that same grace touched thousands in the very city where He had died, met Saul with mercy on his furious road, and has visited this race in everwidening waves of love. Our God is a God of grace who has mercy for all who will come to Him. In Jesus is hope for every situation and cleansing for every sin. We may be like Lazarus — dead, buried and beyond hope, yet even then grace can reach us if we cast at Jesus a look of need.

GOD CONQUERS OUR SIN WITH HIS GRACE

Not only is sin great but it is strong, for it is the devil's bridle on men's wills and the ground of his authority in their lives. Outside God, it is the greatest power in the world today.

The basic power of sin is its power to blind us. The ancients had a cruel yet effective way of dealing with prisoners who were strong or dangerous, like Samson or King Zedekiah. They put their eyes out so as to make them helpless. This is what the devil does — as Paul tells us, "The god of this world hath blinded the minds of them which believe not."[2] Part of this blindness means we cannot see our own sin, so we remain slaves, for what a man cannot see he cannot deal with. The power of sin is its power to blind us to its nature and existence.

But sin also holds us in the power of guilt or condemnation. A man may commit a sin only once yet live ever afterwards under its power because of the shadow of guilt that may darken him to the end of his days. The power of sin is not always the sin itself but what the devil builds upon it. It is not the foundation so much as the superstructure of guilt with its fear of disclosure.

How many a man is weighted down by this? Once we are held by the power of guilt we are truly under sin's power. We may then resort to deceit and unreality or become hard and even self-abandoned. We may go from bad to worse until we come to love our sins and become wedded to them beyond hope of release.

The answer to all this is the grace of God. First He touches our eyes so that we see our sins as they really are. Conviction comes and with it the desire to repent. Then like the blind man whose eyes were anointed to feel his blindness and uncleanness we are told to go and wash.[3]

Dark is the stain we cannot hide;
What can avail to wash it away?
Look, there is flowing a crimson tide,
Whiter than snow you may be today.

GOD DISPLACES OUR SIN WITH HIS GRACE

Sin is not only continually cleansed but is progressively displaced within the life of the Christian. Where sin abounded grace did much more abound, says Paul. This does not mean that God eradicates our sinful nature as a man would uproot one tree and plant another. What He does do, however, is to show us sin more and more clearly and help us to repent on deeper levels so that the hold of sin is loosened and its reign broken within us. God dethrones evil in us and progressively establishes Christ as Lord in its place. Of sin in the Christian, Wesley says, "It *remains,* though it does not *reign.*"[4] It remains however, like King Saul — a rejected monarch whose kingdom must give way more and more before the One whose right it is to reign.

When God meets us with His grace He makes our hearts broken and contrite. He comes to dwell with us, and in so doing sheds His love abroad in our hearts. As He deals with us lovingly about this and that, we find we must turn to Him continually in repentance. We cannot keep away from Him. Like flowers that turn towards the sun because they cannot live unless they receive its light, so we turn lovingly and trustingly to Him and as we do this His grace goes on working in us to pervade and transform us. We are changed from glory to glory. It is a lifelong process, for we are hard to deal with and often turn away. Yet God goes on patiently, working in grace and making us people of grace.

I saw it once in this way. When we are first converted Christ in us is like a tiny white spot in a large circle of black. Where His white touches our black there is contrast, there is conviction of sin followed by repentance and readjustment to Him as He deals with us about many things. But the white spot grows as God gains more place in our life. So does the line of contact. More issues are dealt with and the conflict of grace with sin moves to new areas. We have to repent more, be broken on more matters, and indeed sometimes we may seem to be in a bad way. But all the while, unknown to us, the white circle is growing and the black is shrinking. It is always there and we may be deeply aware of it, but it is on the retreat. Conscious repentance leads us to unconscious holiness as the mighty grace of God meets us, masters us, while Christ who is the grace and power of God within displaces sin by progressively bringing in the victory of His cross and setting up His throne in our hearts. Then it is we can sing:

> *Marvelous grace of our loving Lord;*
> *Grace that exceeds our sin and our guilt.*
> *Yonder on Calvary's mount outpoured;*
> *There where the blood of the Lamb was*
> *   spilt.*
> *Grace, grace, God's grace,*
> *Grace that will pardon and cleanse*
> *   within.*
> *Grace, grace, God's grace,*
> *Grace that is greater than all our sin.*

It is never God's will to leave us mourning over our sins or our sinfulness but ever to lead us to rejoice in the wonder and power of His grace, freely given to us in the sinner's place, through the blood of Christ.

References:
1 - Romans 5:20.
2 - 2 Corinthians 4:4.
3 - John 9:7.
4 - Fifty Three Sermons — No. 13.

7

The way of peace

"Peace, perfect peace, in this dark world of sin?
The blood of Jesus whispers peace within."

*T*he greatest need of many people is for peace.
A psychiatrist tells us that "anxiety is for everyone an indisputable reality of everyday living."[1]
It is a modern curse. The minds of millions today
are strung with tension, hypertension, frustration and fret. It is no wonder, since we have lived
for half a century in a world of fear.

A text-carrier walking the streets of a great
city was once stopped by a lady who pointed at
his sandwich-board and said: "Oh, please give it
to me. I have wanted it for years." "Give you
what?" he asked. "Why, that," she replied, point-
ing to the text on his board. Then he realized the
words were: "Come unto me, and I will give you
rest." How many people like her have been looking for it for years.

HOW WE LOSE OUR PEACE

The prophet Jeremiah spoke of people who
"heal the hurt ... slightly, saying, peace, peace;
when there is no peace."[2] I think most of us are
like this. We give all kinds of reasons for our
unrest of soul. Some of these may be physical.
Our health may be poor or our nerves frayed. It
may be that people get us down or that circumstances are too much for us. Yet none of these

may be the true cause. We may think that if we had a bigger income or a better house or different friends we would have more peace. But we are wrong.

In the year 1930 the late Dr. W.E. Sangster, the Methodist preacher, was in the throes of a spiritual crisis. He wrote in his diary: "I have lost my peace! Thoughts of great unrest have invaded my heart. Part of my unrest probably has a physical basis, but it is by no means wholly of that."[3] We tend to blame many things, *but it is by no means wholly of that.* It is the Bible that tells us how this loss of peace takes place. The answer is there in the story of the first man and the woman God made. As they walked in the garden they were at peace — within themselves, with each other, and with God. Everything was peace in that garden until the serpent came and they listened to him and committed the sin of disobedience. Then came unrest; they lost their peace and began to accuse and blame and hate and kill. A sword of unrest came turning every way. They begat a son who was a wanderer in the earth, and then gave birth to a restless race. Peace went out when sin came in. That is the simple explanation.

Like Adam and Eve we are quick to blame others for our loss of peace. It is the fault of our partner, we say, or the people at the office. It is the weather or the children or the shortage of money. So we blame this and that, failing to see that our unrest stems from other sources, from things such as pride or jealousy, selfishness or unbelief, the same things as the serpent brought in the beginning to that garden of peace. The real trouble is that we want what others have; we grow resentful, we are dragged about by lusts and passions, we allow ourselves to be pulled apart by inward conflicts, so that we are not integrated within ourselves around the right center. We are not at peace with God, so we are not at peace with ourselves and others. We have lost inner poise because of sin, not because of circumstances. The heart that is right with God will have peace, whatever storms may rage outside.

DANGER OF FALSE PEACE

The failure to recognize sin as the basic destroyer of peace leads to a search for wrong solutions. The Puritans called this "false peace", which is what the people of Jeremiah's day looked for as they cried "Peace, Peace" when there was no peace. They healed the hurt lightly, like trying to cure a cancer with a codeine. If we give wrong reasons for our lack of peace, we are bound to look for wrong remedies.

We may seek this false peace along physical lines, taking sedatives or seaside holidays to calm our nerves or bring the color to our cheeks. But if our inner conflicts are not resolved our unrest remains. We may seek along cultural channels, resorting to music, hoping to heal our sadness at her shrine, but music, however divine, will only do what David's harp did for Saul, soothe for a time while it leaves the devil in the soul. The fact is that nothing in human art or culture can deal with basic unrest. For this we need God Himself.

I think the most subtle way of seeking false peace is the religious. Peace is the promise of Christ; it is embedded in our Christian faith and pervades much of our church worship and architecture. Anyone who visits a cathedral knows that. The result is that many find in religion a false peace. A lady once approached me after a church service and said, "Thank you, sir; I came here full of unrest, but I have found such peace in this service." I said, "That is good. Is it peace through the blood of Christ?" She did not understand, so I asked how she had found this peace, and was told it was the reverent service and the beautiful music and singing which had brought peace. But there was no repentance, no sense of forgiveness or inward cleansing. The soothing was momentary; the basic need remained only to give rise later to more unrest. It is a perilous thing to find peace through religion without finding it in Christ Himself who is our Peace. Beware of this false peace! It is a substitute, a parody, a delusion of the devil!

THE SECRET OF TRUE PEACE

True peace is peace with God. It is based on a right relationship with Him, which comes only through forgiveness. There is no other way, for we are sinners needing pardon. P.T. Forsyth says, "We are not merely stray sheep or wandering prodigals, we are rebels taken with weapons in our hands."[4] That means we must be reconciled if we are to have peace, and reconciliation is only by the cross since it was there God did the mighty work of putting away His enmity against us by dealing with the root cause of that enmity, which is our sin against Him. In the atoning death of Christ everything needful was done to take away all vestige of sin from our souls. There is perfect forgiveness for us if we come as sinners who repent. But more, there is the perfect righteousness of Christ for us as well. We can be made as clean as Christ Himself. Here then, is a double cause for us to have peace. Our sins are cleansed and we are made righteous in Christ. All this is for us as sinners — not as good people who come to bargain with God.

Perfect peace is therefore peace for sinners, found in the place where sinners repent. If we want this peace we must cease excusing or blaming and be willing to accept ourselves as the sinners we are. It is this total acceptance of ourselves, this reconciliation with ourselves, this acceptance of God's judgment on ourselves that is so important. Only then can we fully accept Christ and His atoning work for us in its total effect, and be at peace. This is what we mean when we speak of peace through the blood.

In a forest fire there is one place of peace where the flames cannot reach. It is the place where the fire has already burned itself out.

In a forest fire there is one place of peace where the flames cannot reach.

Those who see this and go there find peace. That is what Calvary means, for it is the place where the fire of God's judgment against sin burned itself out completely. There is therefore no condemnation for those who go there in repentance. Pardon and peace are found in the sinner's place.

THE WAY OF PEACE

Like the prodigal son we are always prone to turn away from our Father and go seeking peace in the far country. We need not take long to get there nor need we move far. We have gone wrong somewhere, and the evidence is that we have lost our peace. Like the prodigal the only way is to come back in simple repentance. In returning and resting we are continually saved.

One of the great discoveries of World War II was radar which guided many an aircraft and saved many a crew. It became possible to direct a bomber to a target, even in darkness or bad weather, for the navigator was warned by certain sounds the moment he deviated slightly off course either to the right or left. When he remained on course he remained in peace. This is what the Holy Spirit does in the soul. While we walk with the Lord Jesus we are kept in perfect peace, but the moment we go wrong He convicts us and causes us to lose our peace. The peace of God is like a referee at a football match, who is silent until something is at fault. If we are to recover God's peace we must rediscover God's pardon; we must come again simply and quickly to repent. Then the blood of Jesus will cleanse from all sin and we shall walk with God in peace once more. It is as simple as that.

The One who knows this peace learns to live in it. He becomes sensitive to all that mars fellowship with God, as the human eye reacts to every speck of dust. He learns to repent quickly and come to Christ continually. This is the basic issue of life on which all other issues are settled. He who takes the sinner's place, finds the sinner's peace and knows Jesus to be the sinner's righteousness. His soul is anchored in a harbor from which not all the storms of life can move it.

References:
1 - Guntrip, *Psychology for Ministers and Social Workers.*
2 - Jeremiah 6:14
3 - Doctor W.E. Sangster, Biography, (pp. 90, 91)
4 - *Positive Preaching and the Modern Mind,* p. 56.

8

Personal revival

"In my heart, dear Lord, I pray,
Send a great revival."

The sinner's place is not only the place of acceptance, peace and forgiveness but the place of revival, for it is here where Christ Himself is experienced as the Divine Answer to every need. Revival is a personal thing. It is Jesus Himself coming to us at the point of our need as He came to His disciples in the upper room to meet them in their prison of frustration and fear. Revival is the power of Christ's risen life in us. It was when the disciples were gathered together for fear — then came Jesus.[1]

When Jesus comes to us it is not on the peak of attainment but in the valley of need. This is where the disciples were. "Then came Jesus," and on that experience of His was hinged the destiny of the Church. There would have been no Pentecost, no Gospel, no Church, had He not come back from the dead to stand among His own. They were helpless, futureless men; a guilty Peter, a doubting Thomas, a fearing unbelieving group; yet He came to revive them and set them free.

The trouble with so many of us is that we think we must be good and great and worthy and victorious if we are to experience revival. But it was not so with the disciples. Nor need it be with us. The whole message of this book is that the grace of God, in whatever aspect we know it, is for us at the point of our need and not at the point of our self-sufficiency.

WHAT JESUS FINDS WHEN HE COMES

As the Savior visits our soul, what does He find there? Often He finds disappointment as He did that day He came to the upper room. For years they had followed Jesus looking for a kingdom only to find their hopes shattered. "We trusted," they said, "that it had been He which should have redeemed Israel."[2]   But He had proved a disappointment. Indeed so had they for that matter, for with all their promises and assertions of loyalty they had forsaken Him and fled in the hour of His need.

I wonder if you are a disappointed Christian. There was a time when you intended, even promised much, yet again and again in the moment of testing you have denied Jesus and run away. You feel you have failed miserably to be the Christian you meant to be. Even now you look back on golden days of long ago when your hopes were high and your heart was full of peace and joy. You made the great surrender! It may be you wanted to be a missionary or you served God in some Christian work! Jesus Christ meant everything to you and you would have died for Him. But you are so disappointed today. Somehow those things you believed, hoped, professed have not worked out as you thought. Jesus is a disappointment to you and you are to yourself. Then you are just like those poor disciples.

Perhaps Jesus finds doubt in your soul. He did with the disciples. In fact it was the chief thing He had to deal with after His resurrection. Events had so shaken their faith that when others came telling of what they had seen, they could not believe. "Their words seemed to them as idle tales."[3] Jesus was dead and the kingdom of God laid in ruins.

Does this message come to one like this? You read your Bible but it is like an idle tale! Others speak of Christ but their words are like idle tales! How well do I remember a time when my faith was darkened because I lost faith in other Christians and the light went out of my soul. For weeks I seemed like one slipping on a glacier in the dark, going I knew not where. But then came Jesus! Can I ever forget it? Doubt is a dreadful thing; it is the great destroyer of spiritual peace and joy, the very breath of Satan on the soul. The darkest days of Christian's journey in *Pilgrim's Progress* were when he and his friend were cast into Doubting Castle to be starved and beaten by Giant Despair. Are you in the prison of doubt?

When Jesus came He found defeat. That little group had known such victory as they followed Jesus around. The crowds had been fed, the sick healed, demons had fled and whole towns had been moved to acclamation. They saw the great kingdom of God on the way and themselves reigning on thrones of glory. But when Jesus was taken to Calvary all had been lost. It was only a faded dream.

I believe there are many defeated Christians. They live on the externals of religion, joining with enthusiasm in church services or conventions or evangelistic rallies. They love the ritual and the glamour of it all. They revel in great preaching and the singing of massed choirs. But inside they are defeated Christians knowing nothing of the power of Jesus to save them daily from temper, greed, lust, and pride. How easy it is to be like this — to go with the crowd and look like a victorious Christian when all the while we live defeated in our hearts or our homes.

This kind of thing leads at the last to despair. For that apostolic band there was no hope at all, apart from Christ. The past was shattered into fragments, the future was full of foreboding and the present was, to say the least, uncomfortable. It seemed the devil had won and there was no light left. All these needs led them finally to despair. What changed everything was the discovery that He was alive.

WHAT JESUS DOES WHEN HE COMES

Now, you might think Christ would send some message to these people that they must come out of this terrible room of disappointment, doubt, defeat, and despair to meet Him on the sunny slopes of Olivet. But instead He comes into the room Himself to appear in the midst of it all and so change it by His living presence. They did not have to struggle with their problems. He was Himself the answer.

In one of his books, Mr. C.S. Lewis describes a land wrapped in endless winter by a witch. Everything is hard and cold and the many creatures there live in hopeless fear. But one day a thaw begins, the birds commence to sing and the flowers appear on every hand. It is because Aslan — the great Lion, who is the Son of the great King over the sea, is coming. It is his land and he comes to set it free. The creatures are heard saying, "Aslan is on the move," and then they sing: *"When he shakes his mane, we shall have spring again."*[4]

So the whole scene changes as the Lion advances into the wintry land and the power of the witch is broken.

This is what Christ does. We strive to set ourselves free, thinking we must reach some standard of perfection before He can bless us, when all the time He wants to come to us at the point of our need that He might revive us there. We have already shown how grace is like water flowing from the high reservoir down to the lowest point that our thirst may be quenched. Some friends of mine once found a spring bubbling up in their basement flat. It came from a stream that flowed under their very house. And the wonderful thing about the Lord is that He has power to underflow and undergird our need. He is able to come up in the very midst of our situation even within our poor dry hearts to revive us there. Then came Jesus and stood in

When he shakes his mane, we shall have spring again.

the midst! What a glorious experience is this!

He comes to show *Himself*. It is not a report of Him we need but a revelation. Mere sermons and addresses in themselves will not do. Conferences and conventions are little worth unless our Beloved is there to show Himself to us. What a difference when He appears to our souls. Then the winter is past, the rain is over and gone, the flowers appear and the time of the singing of birds is come. It is revival when Jesus comes. Prayer becomes real and hymns alive with truth; preaching catches fire once more and Christian fellowship takes on a quality unknown before. Doubts are chased away and the prison doors fly open at His touch.

Jesus Himself drew near,
And all their doubts were solved;
He showed them why Christ came to die,
And what that death involved.

This is revival. This is what shines at the heart of every revival — the living Lord Jesus made real to His people in their need.

WHAT JESUS BRINGS WHEN HE COMES

Revival is Jesus bringing the fulness of His life into the emptiness of ours. For every lack in us there is a corresponding grace in Him. He is light for our darkness, life for our death, bread for our hunger, living water for our thirst, rest for our striving, wisdom of God for our foolishness and fellowship for our loneliness. When we see that in Him dwells all the fulness of the Godhead bodily and we can be filled full in Him, then life is changed and our darkness turned to day.[5]

The first words He uttered as He came were words of peace. "Peace be unto you," He said as

He showed them His hands and feet.[6] It was as though He would show them the true source of their peace in the death He had died on the cross. So Jesus would bring you peace by showing you that in His death all your sin has been dealt with. All that underlies your tension and fear can be removed. You can have peace with God — peace about everything. You can live in peace as you walk with Christ in every situation.

Then as He showed them His wounds, He turned their minds away to the world without and said, "As the Father hath sent Me, even so send I you."[7] "Go ye into all the world, and preach the Gospel.[8] It was as though His wounds were windows into the heart of God through which streamed the light of love for mankind. We cannot look into them without feeling the Divine compassion or realizing the cost of man's redemption. A young man who today has as wide a vision as anyone for the rapid reaching of the world with the Gospel, told me how the day Jesus filled his heart in a revival experience he was at once given an impelling urge to evangelize the whole world. So it was with the disciples. So with Paul. So it must be with us. Revival is no locked-up thing. It is a fire that must spread. We cannot know the liberating power of Jesus without longing to go and open the doors of the prison for all mankind.

But we say we are weak and the task is impossible! So did they until Jesus breathed on them and gave them His power. What a momentous thing it was as Jesus went to each of them breathing on them and saying, "Receive ye the Holy Ghost,"[9] as though to give them the very breath with which He did His mighty works on earth, and assure them that this was the first breathing of the great wind of the Holy Spirit who was to come at Pentecost. He can breathe on us — filling us with His own living Spirit, so that it is no longer we who live but Christ who lives in us.

Have you received that Breath of God? If you are a Christian at all then you have. But perhaps He, the Holy Spirit, has ceased to move in you, and the atmosphere of your soul has become stagnant and sultry until you have lost all your spiritual vigor. You have lost your sense of God so that He has become dim and unreal to you. You are poor indeed. You need to be revived. You need to ask Jesus to visit you afresh, to come and show you His hands and side that you might look again into the heart of God and see both the measure of your sin and the greatness of His grace. If you want the fulness of the Holy Spirit you will find it where you find everything else God has to give you — in the sinner's place. There where you see His wounds, you will receive His breath and revival will begin in your heart.

> *When Jesus comes,*
> *the tempter's power is broken;*
> *When Jesus comes,*
> *the night is turned to day.*
> *He takes the gloom*
> *and fills the soul with glory,*
> *For all is changed*
> *when Jesus comes to stay.*

Even so, come Lord Jesus!

*References:*1 - Jn. 20:19;
2 - Luke 24:21;
3 - Luke 24:11;
4 - *The Lion, the Witch and the Wardrobe*
5 - Colossians 2:9, 10;
6 - Luke 24:36;
7 - John 20:21 (R.V.);
8 - Mark 16:15;
9 - John 20:22.

9

The highway of holiness

"If our love were but more simple,
We would take Him at His word,
And our lives would be all sunshine
In the sweetness of the Lord."

In this book we have sought to show a simple way of life in Christ for all who will believe God. Many Christians are confused, for it is a complicated age and we have made the Christian life a tangle of different emphases very different from the simplicity of the Gospel.

I heard once of some boys who, newly converted, went to a Bible class and, not being used to public prayer, found themselves at some loss for words during the chain prayer. At the close an older boy, who was the leader of the class, prayed, "O Lord, we thank You for these new chaps. We know they haven't been Christians very long, so they don't know much. But we know that as they go on with us they will become much more complicated." I am not quite clear what he meant, but he might have said this about many Christians. They were simple when they started, but they have become much more complicated — more than they were ever meant to be.

The prophet Isaiah gives us a picture of the Christian life under the figure of a highway built through a wilderness.[1] Can you see that highway running like a ribbon across the desert where so many people go astray? It is so plain, he tells us, that a wayfaring man, though a fool, need not err therein. You see, the Gospel is not only a doorway *into* life, it is a highway *of* life. As we have received Christ Jesus the Lord so we are to walk in Him. What we found and did at the beginning we are to do throughout. We took a step to Christ which was one of repentance and faith and surrender. Now we are to walk in Him, and a walk in only a reiterated step which may seem simple and even monotonous, but it gets us a long way on the road. So there are certain fundamental things we have emphasized in this book which are the secrets of the true walk with the Lord.

THE SIMPLICITY OF REPENTANCE

Sin can be very complicated. One has only to consider how complex are all the details of a High Court trial to bring to light the one crime of one man, or how tangled are the false motives and desires within our own personalities to see this is so. If we have ever played the game "Chinese Whispers" we know how muddled can be a simple statement once it has passed through a dozen minds. So too a wrong word or act or association can grow into a veritable jungle of confusion amongst a group of people until in the general mass of mankind there seems to be no end to the intricacies of evil.

Because sin is complicated we try to find equally complicated answers. We produce endless arguments and explanations about it. we analyze or excuse until we make the answers to sin more complex than sin itself. Yet all the time there is one simple answer — that of repentance. God has given all the answer needed in the atoning work of Christ on the cross. There is no need for us to go round in endless cycles of explanation and excuse, when all we need to do is repent of the one thing in which we are wrong. We need not be concerned about other people or other issues. Repent of the one thing that is wrong! God will show the next step! This is a simple way, yet it cuts through the Gordian knot and enables God to unravel an otherwise complicated situation.

A six-year-old boy getting out of bed on the wrong side one morning ran straight into trouble. He objected to his clothes and refused to put them on. His breakfast was also wrong so he would not eat it. Having by then annoyed his sisters and crossed his mother, he found himself

His breakfast also was wrong, so he would not eat it.

so tangled up in trouble that his world seemed to be falling about his ears. Finally father came along and said, "Now look, young man; we have had nothing but trouble this morning. What are you going to do about yourself?" There was a pause, then a burst of tears and three pathetic words, "I'm sorry, Daddy," and would you believe it, in two minutes the world was right. The family was reconciled, the tears were wiped away and everything seemed strangely as it should be. All he had done was to repent.

Can you see how simple this is? Then why do we so often refuse to do it? Is it not because pride would make us find other ways? Yet this is often the only way we can take, the only way God wants us to take. This is not to say we take repentance lightly or live only to sin and repent, for if we love the Lord we cannot grieve Him by

In two minutes the world was right.

taking advantage of His grace. Nevertheless since we are sinners we shall ever need the gift of repentance. God has given us a simple way so that, whatever the complications of sin (or of life) may be, there is always liberation and peace for us through the blood of Jesus. As to Israel long ago, God says to us, "Only acknowledge your guilt."[2]

THE SIMPLICITY OF GRACE

Once we have seen the simple way of repentance, the Holy Spirit leads us to see the simplicity of grace. Many people try to live the Christian life by works, like householders who try to find water by sinking a well and pumping when there are taps at hand. Some, like the Galatians,[3] having begun with the taps, have gone over to the pumps. This way of works is very complicated because we feel we have to try, nor can we ever be sure if we have made the grade. It is like one of those "stress dreams" where we climb endless hills with heavy loads only to keep slipping down the slopes. So we fall either into pride or despair.

The way of grace is so simple, like turning on the tap. Let me illustrate! Sometimes I meet people I do not like. Try as I may, I cannot love them. I meet them with a false smile and a niggling sense of hypocrisy. At last I am brought to a place of repentance as God shows me my heart full of unlove and selfishness, lacking the true spirit of Christ. There is nothing I can do but repent — doggedly perhaps. Each time I meet these people there is fresh cause for repentance. But presently I discover in my heart a new love never known before. It comes without effort. Indeed I wonder how I did not love like this before. What has happened? Simply that grace has worked in me. God has done something. He has given me His own love for others — because He has given me Himself. He has laid at my doors the living water of His Spirit from His reservoirs of grace, that I may receive grace and give it to others. That is the way of grace. It *results* in works but it does not first *require* works. It only wants our sense of need, our admission of need. And God being what He is, there is no spiritual need we can have but there is in Christ a corresponding grace for its fulfillment, if we come to Him. This is a most profound thing, but simple enough for a little child.

THE SIMPLICITY OF FELLOWSHIP

The way of repentance and grace leads us into the simple way of fellowship. Again how complicated have we made this. I think it is because sin is complex and so much of our sinning is in relation to one another that fellowship becomes such a tangled affair.

Fellowship is the need of every heart. It is the nature of the Christian life and the church, the atmosphere of God's presence in which we learn and grow into the dimensions of the love of Christ. Fellowship is a simple sweet thing. There is no clearer definition than that of John who says, "If we walk in the light, as He is in the light, we have fellowship one with another, and the blood of Jesus Christ His Son cleanseth us from all sin."[4]

Fellowship comes when we walk in the light. We cannot understand this until we see that "light" in the New Testament is that which reveals or "makes manifest".[5] God is like this. He is holy, transparent, pure, always revealing things as they are. So if we have fellowship with Him we must be willing to be revealed for what we really are. We must walk with Him as sinners, which is why John says we need the blood of Jesus to go on cleansing us. The first thing about fellowship is that we must be real with God; we must let His light show up all our sin.

Our fellowship, however, is with one another, and here too it can only be real as we "walk in the light". This is where we fail for we do not see that our relation with God must work out in our relations with others. If we are unreal and unrepentant towards one another we are hiding part of ourselves which is walking in darkness. The important element in fellowship is reality. The simple process is this: first, we accept ourselves as the people God shows us to be. We admit what we are and walk thus with God. Then we learn that we are accepted by God as we are. He knows us altogether, He has provided for us in Christ, and accepts us in the Beloved. This is the ground of our fellowship with Him. Finally, we learn to accept one another as we are in all the totality of our sinfulness, weakness and need. We do not orbit around one another showing only one face but always hiding the other, as the moon does to the earth. That is not fellowship. Neither do we live on pedestals of reputation looking at one another across the spaces in between.

Some years ago I found myself waiting with a friend on a railway station in a thick fog. As we walked up and down the platform it was impossible to see each other. It was as though we walked in darkness until we came to a place where some men had made a great fire. We found that where it burned the fog was clear, there was warmth and transparency and the nearer we walked to the fire, the more clear we were to each other. Is not this what we need in the church? We are so misted up with unreality in our dealings with one another that we do not know others as they really are, and there is no true fellowship. But when the Holy Spirit burns and we come close to God our unreality has to be dispersed. We stand as sinners together at the cross needing to be cleansed. Then true love shines, we find it easy to share with and trust one another as we repent together and find grace in the sinner's place. We grow to understand and feel safe with one another. There is nothing so sweet on earth as this simple fellowship of Christians who repent. Jesus stands among us shedding His holy light until it seems that nothing evil or unreal can linger there. It becomes easy to repent but hard to hurt one another. Our hearts are melted together and we could lay down our lives for the brethren.

This is the kind of fellowship God seeks to create and Christians need to know everywhere today. How much lack of love there is for one another! How much absence of caring that leaves many in loneliness, dryness and need! How different it could be, for there is nothing complicated about this way of fellowship. It needs no great organization or technique, for it is simply the Lord Himself blessing us together as we allow Him to cleanse us of the sins that divide. If we will be real with Him and one another, then He will be real to us. This is the answer to the division of the world and the church, the answer to the hunger of the human heart.

THE SIMPLICITY OF REVIVAL

I must conclude with a word on the great question of spiritual awakening which is in the minds of so many today. At the heart of revival — any revival — there is one great event. Ecstasies and activities, data and phenomena there may be, but at the heart of revival is Christ made known to repenting sinners. Paul tells us in the first chapter of Ephesians of the great power and glory of Christ — how He is risen far above all, how all things are beneath His feet, so that He fills everything.[6] Then having described Him thus, he says that He (God) "gave Him to the church". He is *for* the church — for you and me! Why then should we be poor and weak and frustrated when He who is the very fulness of God is all for us? Everything in Christ is for us … wisdom, righteousness, holiness, liberation. He can meet us in His limitless resurrection life, every day of our life and set us gloriously free.

The Christian life is a walk. It is a progressive relation with God in Christ, in which every need of ours is related to Him and His grace given us in exchange. It is a way of repentance and brokenness which becomes a way of grace and peace. This in turn becomes a way of fellowship and of spiritual life and power. Here is Isaiah's picture of the highway along which we walk together with God.

The highway stretches on through the wilderness of life with all its confusing issues. It may be you feel you need God at this time. You need to be revived spiritually. You pray that He would work in your church or fellowship where things seem dead and dry. You are confused by many religious emphases. Here is the way of simplicity, the life in which you come day by day to Christ in brokenness, repentance, reality, to take from Him His cleansing, grace, peace and fellowship. You hear His voice saying, "This is the way, walk ye in it,"[7] and as you come to walk with Him you find He begins to work in you, as He did long ago when He talked with the two on the Emmaus Road. And now let me ask if you will be simple enough to walk with Christ as a repenting sinner on the highway of grace and holiness. If you do you will find it a highway of life and glory and revival will have begun in your soul.

References:
1 - Isaiah 35:8
2 - Jeremiah 3:13 (R.S.V.)
3 - Galatians 3:3
4 - I John 1:7
5 - Ephesians 5:13
6 - Ephesians 1:22
7 - Isaiah 30:21.

101 Ways to Change Your World

Geoff Tunnicliffe
ISBN: 1-884543-47-2

Geoff Tunnicliffe has compiled an invaluable collection of ways to change the world in his newly revised *101 Ways to Change Your World*. In addition to 101 practical ways to put faith into action, Tunnicliffe has also included statistics and resources for individuals desiring to make a difference in God's World.

God's Great Ambition

Dan & Dave Davidson
George Verwer
ISBN: 1-884543-69-3

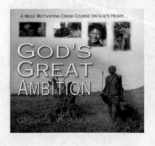

This unique collection of quotes and Scriptures has been designed to motivate thousands of people into action in world missions. George Verwer and the Davidsons are well-known for their ministries of mission mobilization as speakers and writers. Prepare to be blasted out of your comfort zone by this spiritual dynamite!

Operation World
21st Century Edition
Patrick Johnstone & Jason
Mandryk
ISBN: 1-85078-357-8

The definitive prayer handbook for the church is now available in its 21st Century Edition containing 80% new material! Packed with informative and inspiring fuel for prayer about every country in the world, *Operation World* is essential reading for anyone who wants to make a difference! Over 2,000,000 in print!

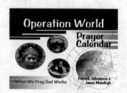

Operation World Prayer Calendar
ISBN: 1-884543-59-6
Spiral-bound desktop perpetual format

Containing clear graphics and useful geographic, cultural, economic and political statistics on 122 countries of the world, the *Operation World Prayer Calendar* is a fantastic tool to help you pray intelligently for the world. Pray for each country for three days and see how God works!

Operation World Wall Map
Laminated or Folded

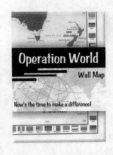

This beautiful, full-color wall map is a great way to locate the countries each day that you are praying for and build a global picture. Not only an excellent resource for schools, churches and offices but a valuable tool for the home.

Dr. Thomas Hale's Tales of Nepal

Living Stones of the Himalayas
(1-884543-35-9)
Don't Let the Goats Eat the Loquat Trees
(1-884543-36-7)
On the Far Side of Liglig Mountain
(1-884543-34-0)

These fascinating accounts of the true-life stories of doctors Tom and Cynthia Hale share everyday and incredible experiences of life with the beguiling character and personalities of the Nepalese people. In sharing these experiences the reader is truly transported to a most enchanting land.